NIPPON

*Land
of Beauty
and Tradition*

NIPPON

Land of Beauty and Tradition

Text   Philip Sandoz

Photographs   Narumi Yasuda

CHARLES E. TUTTLE COMPANY
Rutland, Vermont & Tokyo, Japan

Published by the Charles E. Tuttle Company, Inc.
of Rutland, Vermont & Tokyo, Japan
with editorial offices at
2-6 Suido 1-chome, Bunkyo-ku, Tokyo 112

Library of Congress Catalog Card No. 92-82612
International Standard Book No. 0-8048-1855-x

First edition, 1992

Printed in Japan

The Publisher would like to thank Mr. Takeshi Kojima for his photographs of the fall foliage on page 26 and the geisha on page 32.

CAPTIONS

p. 1 (half title) Cherry blossoms, Chion'in, Kyoto

pp. 2-3 Rice harvest, Miyagi Prefecture

pp. 4-5 (title page) Sumiyoshi Shrine, Osaka

p. 6 Chrysanthemums, Tokyo

p. 72 Carp streamers, Tokyo

Contents

Map of Japan	8		THE JAPAN ALPS	44
Introduction	10		*Backbone of Japan*	
TOKYO	12		TOHOKU	48
The Nation's Capital			*The Northern Prefectures*	
MOUNT FUJI	20		KYUSHU	54
Symbol of Japan			*Gateway to the Outside World*	
KYOTO	24		HOKKAIDO	58
Source of the Nation's Spirit			*The Last Frontier*	
NARA	34		HIDDEN DESTINATIONS	62
The Ancient Capital			*Off the Beaten Track*	
THE INLAND SEA	38		LAND OF FOLK CRAFTS	68
Channel of Commerce and Culture			*Dolls in All Shapes and Styles*	

Facts About Japan

AREA: 145,874 sq. mi. (377,815 sq. km.)

ELEVATION: *Highest* – Mt. Fuji 12,388 ft. (3,776m.)
 Lowest – sea level

CAPITAL: Tokyo

POPULATION: 123,800,000. *Density* – 849 persons per sq. mi. (328 persons
 per sq. km.)

LANGUAGE: Japanese

RELIGIONS: Shintoism, Buddhism

FORM OF GOVERNMENT: Constitutional monarchy. *Symbol of state* – emperor.
 Head of government – prime minister

LITERACY RATE: 99 percent

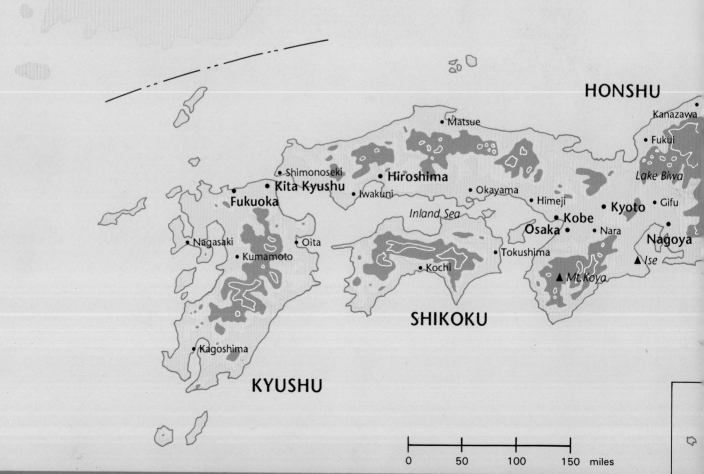

SOUTH KOREA

HONSHU

Kanazawa

Fukui

Matsue

Lake Biwa

Shimonoseki

Hiroshima

Kita Kyushu

Iwakuni

Okayama

Himeji

Kyoto

Gifu

Fukuoka

Inland Sea

Kobe

Osaka

Nara

Nagasaki

Oita

Nagoya

Kumamoto

Tokushima

▲ Ise

Kochi

▲ Mt. Koya

SHIKOKU

Kagoshima

KYUSHU

0   50   100   150   miles

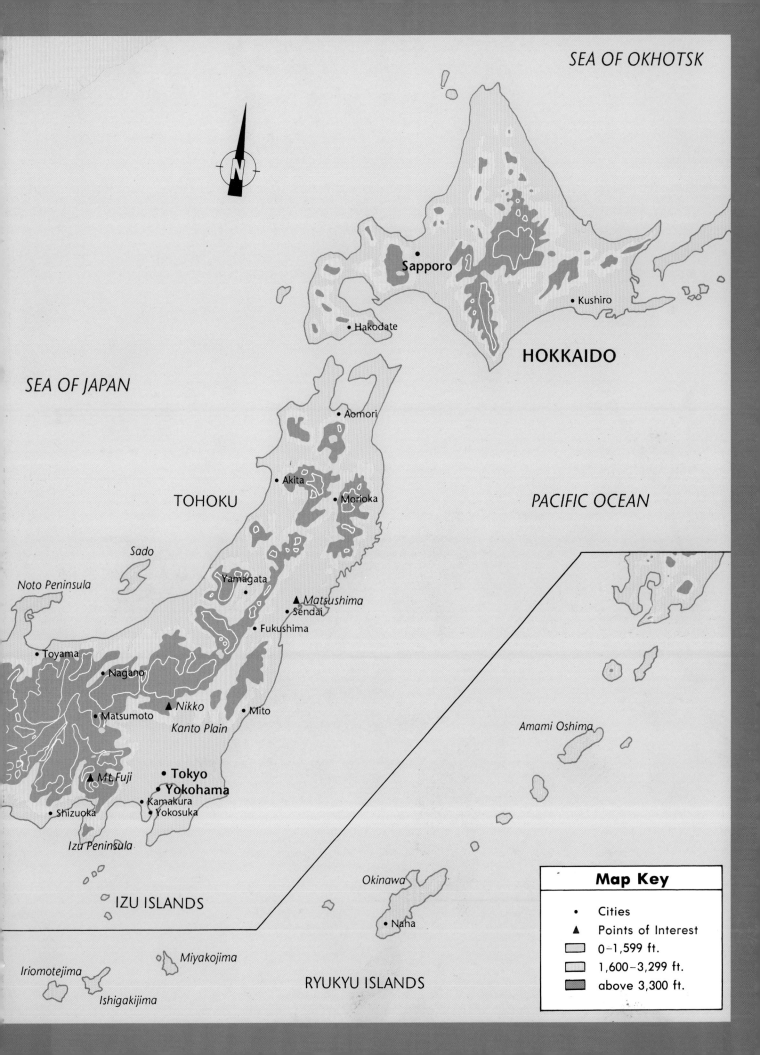

SEA OF OKHOTSK

• Sapporo

• Kushiro

• Hakodate

HOKKAIDO

SEA OF JAPAN

• Aomori

• Akita

TOHOKU

• Morioka

PACIFIC OCEAN

Sado

Noto Peninsula

Yamagata •

▲ Matsushima
• Sendai

• Fukushima

• Toyama

• Nagano

▲ Nikko

• Mito

• Matsumoto

Kanto Plain

Amami Oshima

▲ Mt. Fuji

• **Tokyo**
• **Yokohama**
• Kamakura
• Yokosuka

• Shizuoka

Izu Peninsula

Okinawa

IZU ISLANDS

• Naha

Miyakojima

Iriomotejima

RYUKYU ISLANDS

Ishigakijima

Map Key

• Cities

▲ Points of Interest

☐ 0–1,599 ft.

☐ 1,600–3,299 ft.

☐ above 3,300 ft.

Introduction

On first visiting Japan, Westerners are often surprised because apocryphal tales and even accurate statistics belie the reality, variety, and beauty of this long, narrow archipelago. The entire land mass of Japan could fit into the state of Montana with enough room left over for three and a half Rhode Islands. Within this area, however, are packed almost 124 million people (Montana has around 787,000) and an amazing diversity of climatic conditions.

From the bitterness of Japan's northernmost point, Bentenjima, at almost the same latitude as the Siberian city of Khabarovsk, to the tropical atmosphere of Yonaguni-jima, a metaphorical stone's throw from Taiwan, Nippon encompasses every possible gradation of climate and topography.

The Japanese people, their traditions, beliefs, and ways of life are equally diverse. Almost every Westerner knows of Sony, Nissan, Toshiba, and Nintendo; many have even heard about Shinto, cherry-blossom viewing, shoguns, and Kabuki; but few connect Japan with sun-bronzed islanders lounging beneath palm trees, hunters tracking and trapping wild boars and bears through untouched wildernesses, or the lone farmer driving his harvester through vast fields of ripe, golden wheat.

Japan is all this, and much, much more. The country's 250 years of isolation from the outside world during the Edo period is well known, but often forgotten are the thousands of years of early Japanese civilization, influenced strongly by the culture of the larger nations to the west, predominantly China, which introduced writing, rice cultivation, and Confucianism, and India, the source of Buddhism. Even today, as any visitor will see, foreign influences on Japanese culture and lifestyle continue as strong as ever, proving that isolationism was the exception rather than the rule.

Nippon: Land of Beauty and Tradition introduces many of Japan's most spectacular sites and scenes, and is certain to bring back a host of memories for those who have visited Japan. And the armchair traveler too will be taken on a thoroughly pleasing tour of one of the world's most beautiful and fascinating countries.

TOKYO

The Nation's Capital

Five thousand years ago, the handful of hunter-gatherers who left behind the shell mounds unearthed in Tokyo's Shinagawa ward could not have dreamed that they would be the forerunners of today's twelve million inhabitants of one of the world's industrial, commercial, and financial powerhouses. What they did no doubt recognize, however, were the geographic and climatic conditions that seeded Tokyo's growth from a tiny fishing hamlet, first recorded in 1457, to the bustling metropolis it has become today.

Situated on a wide, fertile coastal plain, what is now Tokyo and its surroundings would have provided the primitives with an abundance of food, sufficient building and clothing materials, and freedom from the rugged, forbidding mountains that reign supreme over 70 percent of Japan's total area. Even now, 7 percent of the country is considered inaccessible.

Today Tokyo is a remarkably international city, with ample provisions of everything the Westerner or Easterner could possibly want, but it is ironic that the city's rise to prominence and then dominance of the country came during the Edo period (1603–1868), when the Tokugawa shoguns strangled development with a garrote of feudalism and isolationism. With the restoration to power of Emperor Meiji in 1868 came the rush for modernization and westernization that has made Greater Tokyo a complex and enticing medley of traditional Japanese culture and international influences.

A single day's trip around the capital city clearly reveals Tokyo's rich diversity. From Asakusa Kannon Temple with its classic Kaminarimon gate (left) to the forty-eight-story, ultramodern Tokyo City Hall; from the manic hustle and bustle of the shopping centers of Shibuya, Ikebukuro, and Ginza to the serene peace of Meiji Shrine and Shinjuku Gyoen National Garden; from the financial frenzy of the Tokyo Stock Exchange to the minor wheelings and dealings of myriad flea markets, Greater Tokyo today tempts resident and visitor alike with a kaleidoscopic world of past and present.

ABOVE
Tokyo's new City Hall, designed by world-acclaimed architect Kenzo Tange, stands as a tribute to the city's wealth and power.

LEFT
This gingko-lined avenue provides the perfect shady walk from trendy Aoyama to the National Sports Stadium.

RIGHT
In late spring, visitors can experience the intoxicating beauty of the irises in the gardens of Meiji Shrine.

ABOVE
For most Japanese, the new year starts with a
pilgrimage to a shrine.

BELOW
This flea market in Tokyo's Setagaya ward has
been held for over four hundred years.

The Shichi-go-san (seven-five-three) festival brings tradition-ally clad boys of five and girls of seven and three to shrines to pray for good luck.

Without a doubt, the most enthusiastically celebrated tradition in Japan is cherry-blossom viewing. Each spring Tokyo's Ueno Park plays host to thousands of picnickers eating, drinking, and singing the balmy evenings away under the mag-nificent pink canopy.

ABOVE LEFT
One of Japan's most famous statues of the Buddha is in Kamakura. Almost forty feet tall and cast in 1252, the bronze statue bears testament to the technological ability and refined artistry of the ancient Japanese.

LEFT
The beauty of Japanese architecture is often encapsulated in the gentle, flowing lines of Buddhist temples like Chuzenji in Nikko.

ABOVE
Japan's indigenous religion, Shinto, is the source of many elaborate spectacles, such as this procession at Nikko's Toshogu Shrine in memory of former shogun Tokugawa Ieyasu.

RIGHT
Japan is not all Buddhism and Shintoism. Yokohama's Chinatown could be called a temple of the best in Chinese cuisine.

MOUNT FUJI

Symbol of Japan

A popular Japanese saying reflects both the spiritual importance of Fuji-san, Mount Fuji, to the Japanese and the pragmatic approach they have to religions of all kinds: Every man should climb Fuji-san once, but anyone who does it twice is a fool.

Each year in July and August over a million people of all ages scale the 12,388-foot volcano in what has become a mixture of pilgrimage and family outing. As one approaches the still technically active volcano, it is impossible not to stare in awe at its grandeur and simple beauty. Presiding over the Fuji-Hakone-Izu National Park, Fuji-san sweeps grandly up from its necklace of lakes to a gentle, classic volcanic cone, in a magnificence that can probably be compared only with Tanzania's Mount Kilimanjaro.

Fuji-san has long been revered as a sacred mountain and a home of the gods. Its name is believed to predate the Japanese language, being derived from the word for fire of the Ainu, the indigenous people of Japan. From the twelfth century until the Meiji Restoration in 1868, Buddhist theology claimed that Fuji-san was a gateway to another world, and, like other natural shrines, it was off limits to women. In modern times, however, though still retaining its mystical aura, Fuji-san is viewed as a symbol of the nation and the heart of the vacation area most convenient for Tokyoites, women included.

Less than three hours from Tokyo by public transportation, the Fuji-Hakone-Izu National Park covers 472 square miles, including parts of Yamanashi, Shizuoka, and Kanagawa prefectures, and provides easy access to some of the most scenic mountains, lakes, beaches, and hot-spring resorts in the entire country. The beauty of the park can be enjoyed throughout the year, with highlights being the spring azalea and peach blossoms (left), the summer climbing and water-skiing seasons, the New England-like magnificence of the fall leaves, and, in winter, the sight of snowcapped Fuji-san towering majestically over the frozen plain below.

RIGHT
This view of the Shuzenji temple in Shizuoka Prefecture attests to the gorgeous autumn colors in the Izu Peninsula.

BELOW
The cultivation of Japan's favorite beverage, green tea, relies on methods that have gone unchanged for centuries.

BELOW RIGHT
Ashinoko, near Mount Fuji, is one of Japan's most beautiful lakes and most popular vacation spots. Traditional hotels and hot-spring resorts abound in the area.

KYOTO

Source of the Nation's Spirit

In A.D. 794, Kyoto, or Heiankyo (Capital of Peace), as it was then known, was founded as the new capital of Japan by Emperor Kammu. For the next 1,100 years, a period marked by bloody civil wars and the rise and fall of several lines of rulers, Kyoto would remain the home of the imperial court, the seat of religious authority, and the wellspring of Japanese culture. The city and its environs today, mercifully spared the widespread destruction of World War II, still provide the visitor with tantalizing glimpses of the cultured, literate, civilized Japan that existed for over a thousand years before Commander Matthew Perry and his Black Ships opened Japan to Western influences in 1853.

Kyoto today remains filled with all sorts of architectural structures that attest to the city's remarkable history. One such place is Nijo Castle, where Kyoto's imperial legacy and feudal past are both readily apparent. The castle contains numerous spectacular works of art but is probably best characterized by corridors specifically built with floors that creaked when walked upon by would-be assassins, an audible reminder of the strife that continued during the centuries that Kyoto served as the cradle, school, and college of Japanese culture.

Much of Kyoto's glory, though often associated with certain distinguished emperors, is actually due to the influences of Buddhism, which has been an important force in the country's development for over 1,200 years, most of which time Kyoto served as the capital of Japan. As a result, many of Japan's greatest art treasures are found in the city's 1,500 temples.

Even in the late twentieth century, Kyoto continues to exert its influence on the spirituality of the Japanese, with thirty of the city's temples remaining the centers of various Buddhist sects, and over two hundred Shinto shrines being located within the city limits. One of Kyoto's most famous shrines is Fushimi Inari, approached by a narrow pathway lined with a thousand brightly painted torii (left) that lead visitors toward the shrine's inner sanctuary.

ABOVE
Kyoto's Kiyomizudera, one of the city's most famous temples, is enchanting during any season.

LEFT
Japanese architecture is designed to harmonize with the landscape and blend in with the changing seasons.

RIGHT
Kinkakuji, or the Golden Pavilion, one of Japan's most gorgeous sights, reflects the early morning sun.

ABOVE

A blanket of moss adds a luxurious touch to the peaceful surroundings of Sanzen'in in Kyoto's Ohara district.

BELOW
Few places can match the serene beauty of
Ryoanji's enigmatic rock garden.

Ancient stone buddhas nestle in the shade on the grounds of the Daikakuji temple.

ABOVE
The peaceful appearance of Kyoto's Teradaya inn masks its dramatic past, which included a confrontation between rival Kyushu factions that left seven samurai dead.

LEFT
Maiko, apprentice geisha, perform the traditional tea ceremony in a Kyoto teahouse.

RIGHT
The area near the Togetsukyo bridge in Arashiyama, Kyoto, is famed for its cherry blossoms and autumn foliage.

NARA

The Ancient Capital

In the mists of prehistory and myth, Japan is said to have been founded by legendary Emperor Jimmu in the Yamato Basin (now Nara), and for many centuries afterward the capital city was changed on the demise of each successive emperor. It was not until Empress Gemmei came to the throne that a permanent capital was established in Heijokyo, today's Nara, in A.D. 710.

The city's overall design shows more Chinese character than any other major city in Japan, due to the fact that Nara was laid out on a rectangular grid modeled very closely on the T'ang capital of Ch'ang-an (modern Xian).

During its mere seventy-four years as the seat of government, Nara forever influenced Japanese culture through the introduction and propagation of Buddhism, and the creation of a number of the country's earliest and greatest literary works, including the *Kojiki* and the *Nihon Shoki*, historical chronicles of ancient Japan, and the *Fudoki*, the earliest physical description of the country.

Today one of the most famous and impressive features of the city is Nara Park, containing 1,300 acres of beautifully wooded landscapes, the five-story pagoda of Horinji (left), Sarusawa Pond, and herds of tame roe deer that charm visitors.

A visit to Tamukeyama-Hachiman Shrine may provide the visitor with some understanding of Japan's current strength in technology. The shrine, founded in 749, was built with a technique that was an early version of air conditioning. The construction is based on wooden sections joined together without nails. When the humidity rises, the wooden sections expand and prevent the entry of warm, wet air, but when the air is dry, the wood contracts, allowing a flow of cooling air into the building. The unique construction at least partly accounts for the wonderful state of preservation of the many works of art the shrine contains, some more than a thousand years old. One of Nara's most famous architectural treasures is also over a thousand years old. Horyuji, completed in 607, is the oldest surviving temple in Japan and one of the oldest wooden structures in the world.

LEFT
Over 1,100 years ago, the Kasuga festival was started in honor of the emperor.

BELOW LEFT
The immense Todaiji monastery and temple house a fifty-three-foot-tall bronze Buddha.

RIGHT
The Japanese love of flowers creates breath-taking sites like wisteria-hung Kasuga Shrine.

BELOW
It is sunset over the pond near the tomb of Emperor Sujin, who reigned almost 2,100 years ago.

THE INLAND SEA

Channel of Commerce and Culture

Bounded by Japan's largest island of Honshu on the north and the east, Kyushu on the west, and Shikoku on the south, the Inland Sea, or Seto Naikai, also forms the Inland Sea National Park. With a maximum width of 248 miles and a maximum north-south distance of forty-three miles, the park includes a picturesque, irregular shoreline and over a thousand islands, many uninhabited and clothed only in bamboo or red pine. The sea itself, though dangerous due to strong tidal movements and treacherous currents, rarely reaches a depth of more than 130 feet.

Today the region is mainly known as a beautiful tourist area, but the Inland Sea played an important part in Japan's feudal history. In 1185, the country's two strongest families, the Tairas and the Minamotos, fought a vicious naval battle in the western part of the Inland Sea for control of the country. The Minamoto family emerged victorious but at a great cost: the loss of the imperial jewels and sword, which sank to the bottom of the sea, where they still, no doubt, lie waiting for an intrepid adventurer to restore them to the country. One ancient treasure of the Inland Sea area that has survived to the present day is Himeji Castle (left), also called the Egret Castle, due to its resemblance to that graceful white bird. Himeji Castle is one of the finest examples of castle architecture in Japan.

The Inland Sea served as an important trade conduit between the former capitals of Kyoto and Nara and the island of Kyushu, as well as an early base of international trade between Japan, Korea, and China. And this same sea also played an integral part in the country's religious history, as witnessed by a large number of shrines and temples, like Kotohira, in northern Shikoku, and Miyajima, south of Hiroshima.

Since World War II the area has seen remarkable growth, with contacts greatly increased by the opening of the Seto Ohashi Bridge linking Honshu with Shikoku. Even with this development, however, the overwhelming character of the Inland Sea remains a beautiful reminder of ancient Japan and its reliance on waterborne trade.

PREVIOUS PAGES
Itsukushima Shrine, on the island of Miyajima, is dedicated to deities who protect sailors.

RIGHT
At the Shitennoji temple in Osaka, young men in loincloths join in the frenzy of a *hadaka*, or naked, festival, a rite of purification and renewal.

ABOVE RIGHT
The classic simplicity of Japanese architecture is typified by the arched bridge in Kuribayashi Park in Kagawa Prefecture.

BELOW RIGHT
The marvel of modern Japanese technology is shown by the Seto Ohashi Bridge linking the formerly sleepy island of Shikoku with Japan's main island of Honshu.

ABOVE
Kobe retains many nineteenth-century, Western-style houses originally built for foreign traders.

RIGHT
The Atomic Bomb Dome in Hiroshima is a stark reminder of the horrors of war.

THE JAPAN ALPS

Backbone of Japan

Japan, the land of electronics, computers, and crowds, is also remarkable for its wild, unspoiled areas of natural beauty. The Japan Alps are reminiscent of the Alps of central Europe, both in topography and high levels of winter snowfall. However, the similarity finishes there. The Japan Alps have not as yet been overcivilized by centuries of tourists, and are still the habitat of wild boars, ptarmigan, and mountain antelopes. Furthermore, unlike the European Alps, the Japan Alps still contain many active volcanoes, which admittedly give rise to avalanches but also to the natural hot springs that provide the perfect relaxing end to a day's hiking or skiing.

Though currently undergoing rapid development as a tourist area, much of the region has changed little since it entranced English visitors in the late nineteenth century, eventually being made famous by Walter Weston, the "father of Japanese mountaining," in his *Mountaineering and Exploration in the Japanese Alps* (1896).

Two places not to be missed, even if visited only on day trips, are the Kamikochi Valley and the city of Takayama. Kamikochi is ideal for the casual hiker. Surrounded by a series of magnificent mountains, the Kamikochi Valley follows the Azusa River and is best viewed from the Kappa Bridge (left), which forms the base for several well-charted walks of between two and four hours through some of the most beautiful countryside anywhere in the world.

Takayama, though now a center of tourism, typifies Japan's old-world charm, with the visitor still able to visit many old houses and watch demonstrations of traditional crafts, including carpentry, pottery making, and lacquerware making. Former Japanese lifestyles can also be glimpsed by a visit to the Kusakabe Mingeikan, a traditional-style house of a nineteenth-century merchant, and a walk through the Sanmachi-suji, three tiny streets in the center of town lined with old wooden houses and shops. And a mere hour or so away from Takayama are the famous farmhouses of Shirakawa, their roofs steeply angled to prevent snow from accumulating during the region's harsh winters.

ISHIKAWA
• Kanazawa
TOYAMA
• Nagano
▲ Yarigatake 10,433
NAGANO
• Takayama
GIFU
• Matsumoto
▲ Kitadake 10,472
YAMANASHI
▲ Mt. Fuji 12,388
SHIZUOKA
• Shizuoka

ABOVE
Mount Minami Koma-
gatake towers in
splendor above other
peaks in the Japan Alps.

RIGHT
The ancient Nakasendo
highway, linking Tokyo
and Kyoto, is now just
a meandering byway.

BELOW
Wasabi, Japanese horse-
radish, is largely culti-
vated in Nagano
Prefecture.

RIGHT
Gifu Prefecture's
Takayama area boasts
many fine examples of
traditional Japanese
architecture.

TOHOKU

The Northern Prefectures

Toward the end of the eighth century a battle was about to take place between two clans fighting for control of Tohoku, now consisting of the six prefectures of Aomori, Akita, Iwate, Yamagata, Miyagi, and Fukushima, but at that time a wild, violent area not yet settled or controlled. In the city of Aomori, now the capital of Aomori Prefecture, Sakanoue no Tamuramaro, the leader of one clan, realized that he was probably fatally outnumbered, and devised a plan that today provides good reason for visiting the area. As darkness fell, he ordered large, illuminated papier-mâché figures to be carried around the town to fool the enemy about the size and disposition of his troops. This ploy is still celebrated every year on August evenings when huge, beautiful figures are paraded through the streets of Aomori and other Tohoku cities to the delight of residents and visitors alike.

There are many other reasons to visit Tohoku, not the least being the region's rustic simplicity and relative isolation. Still a predominantly rural area, which produces 20 percent of the nation's rice crop as well as vast amounts of other foods, Tohoku is only now becoming a popular tourist destination, attracting visitors with colorful festivals like Sendai's Tanabata Matsuri, historical treasures like Hiraizumi's glittering Golden Hall, and magnificent scenery like Iwate Prefecture's rugged Rikuchu Coast (left).

Recent improvements in road, rail, and air links have opened up the area to winter sports lovers, heading for, among many other sites, the seven peaks of Mount Zao in Yamagata Prefecture, where some of Japan's best skiing can be experienced. Also beckoned by Tohoku are lovers of the traditional Japan that still exists in the hundreds of small towns and villages that have been cut off by mountains for centuries.

Perhaps the centuries of isolation, as well as the climate, are also responsible for the belief held strongly by almost all Japanese men that the most beautiful women in the country are to be found in remote Akita Prefecture. After all, the unattainable is often considered the most desirable.

The darkness of approaching storm clouds contrasts with the bright gold of these Tohoku rice fields.

LEFT
Participants in the Uesugi shrine festival, held in Yonezawa, Yamagata Prefecture in May, wear costumes from Japan's feudal past.

BELOW
Thatched farmhouses are still relatively common in rural Yamagata Prefecture.

RIGHT
Old ways of living and farming are preserved in the Tono area of Iwate Prefecture.

KYUSHU

Gateway to the Outside World

Kyushu, Japan's southernmost main island, has for more than two thousand years welcomed and suffered from the introduction and propagation of foreign influences. As early as the second century B.C., contact had been made with China, from where rice cultivation was introduced. In the second half of the thirteenth century, Kyushu bore the brunt of two attempted naval invasions by Mongol leader Kublai Khan, both attacks thwarted by typhoons, or, as the Japanese came to call them, *kamikaze*, literally "divine wind."

In the sixteenth century a small section of the port of Nagasaki was opened to foreign traders, predominantly Portuguese, Dutch, and Spanish, who initiated Japan's trade with the Philippines, Goa, and ultimately Europe.

The seventeenth century produced one of the first recorded Western views of Japan, *History and Description of Japan*, written by Engelbert Kaempfer, a German resident of Nagasaki, who actually visited the shogun's court, where he was regarded as an exotic curiosity and forced to sing and dance.

With the arriving European traders also came Christian missionaries, led by the Jesuits. The Japanese isolationist shogunate of the time began to fear the spread of Christianity, and in 1597 twenty-six Christian martyrs were crucified in Nagasaki. Christianity, however, was not to be eradicated, as shown today by the presence of a number of churches, including Nagasaki's Urakami Catholic Church (left).

Despite numerous false starts and isolationist controls, Kyushu has remained the heart of foreign influence in Japan, and today is the home of various arts and industries based on knowledge gained first from contacts with China and Korea and afterwards with Western nations. Notable examples are pottery making and the production of semiconductors.

Kyushu today provides the visitor with a microcosm of modern Japan. High-tech industry and traditional agriculture live side by side, and crowded cities coexist with a classically beautiful countryside of sleepy hamlets, verdant rice fields, and natural hot springs.

ABOVE
The mansion of Thomas Blake Glover, over-looking Nagasaki Bay, was the original setting for Puccini's *Madame Butterfly*.

ABOVE
Kagoshima's sand baths are believed to be extremely beneficial to health.

BELOW
The Ube shrine clings to the steep cliff side in Miyazaki Prefecture.

The active volcano Sakurajima, in Kagoshima, is the source of many natural hot springs.

HOKKAIDO

The Last Frontier

Hokkaido, the northernmost of Japan's four main islands, is a refreshing surprise to the visitor. Though lying slightly farther south than Florence, Italy, the island is more reminiscent of Canada, Scotland, or Scandinavia, which is not surprising, since only the Soya Strait divides it from the Siberian island of Sakhalin. Making up almost 22 percent of Japan's total land mass, Hokkaido bears the weight of only 5 percent of the country's population, enjoying open space and natural beauty rarely encountered in Japan's crowded and industrialized islands.

Hokkaido has long been the domain of the Ainu, the indigenous people of Japan who still live in certain parts of the island. Although the island's early history tends to mirror the development of the main island of Honshu, Hokkaido was not really considered a part of Japan proper until the Edo period (1603–1868), when the first Japanese settlers colonized the southernmost peninsula.

After the Meiji Restoration of 1868, the new government encouraged the economic development of Hokkaido as a means of increasing the output of agricultural products and raw materials. Original plans were for a rapid development of Hokkaido, but in 1881 a major scandal arose when the government, after considerable investment, decided to sell off to its patrons all its holdings in the island for a pittance. When the facts were made known, a public uprising forced the government to rescind its plans, and development of the island slowed down. This incident, plus the colder, drier climate, unlike that of all other areas of Japan, and the vast areas of mountains and virgin forest, probably prevented Hokkaido from becoming simply another Honshu, and gave it the unique character it retains to this day.

Hokkaido is definitely Japan's last frontier, with an open feeling and geography not unlike that of the old American West. Vast rolling wheat fields (left) complement forests of wild animals, which neighbor clear, ice-cold lakes, active volcanoes, and natural hot springs, providing the visitor with something not usually expected of Japan.

LEFT
Cranes, native to Hokkaido, are a symbol of longevity in Japan, according to one proverb, living for a thousand years.

BELOW
Summers in Hokkaido are sunny and dry, but the debt is repaid by cold, snowy winters.

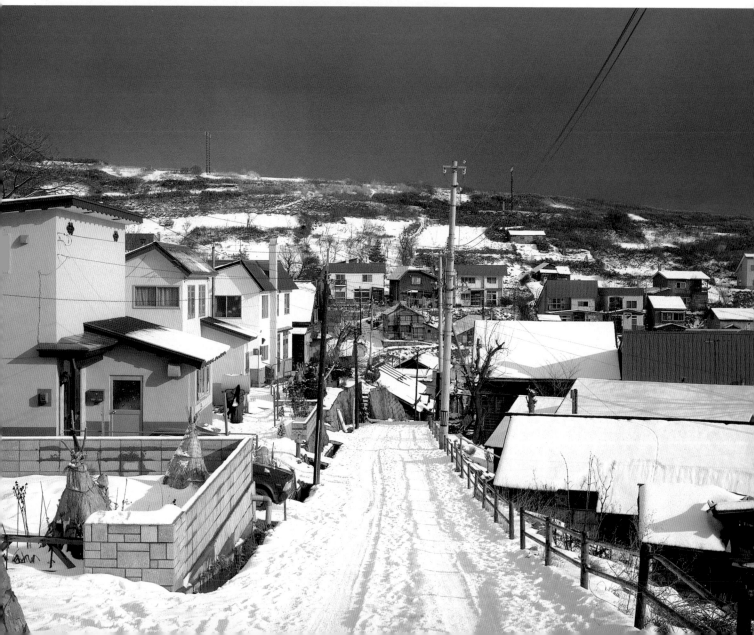

RIGHT
The Sapporo Yuki Matsuri, a
festival featuring gigantic snow
and ice sculptures, is held
annually in February.

BELOW
Though Hokkaido provides
much of Japan's agricultural
output, most farms are still small,
family-run enterprises.

HIDDEN DESTINATIONS

Off the Beaten Track

From the moment the foreign visitor steps off the plane at Narita, the strongest impressions of Japan are the never-ending crowds and the almost intolerable noise levels. Nowhere, it seems, can one be alone with one's thoughts, surrounded by silence. At many tourist destinations armies of grandmothers battle shoals of school children to get a glance at the sights before they are blocked by snaking lines of organized tours. All are shepherded about by whistle-blowing guides and ordered where to go, where not to go, what to do, what not to do. But this is the Japan that, with a minimum of planning and imagination, can be avoided.

In reality, few countries of Japan's size (and many much larger) can offer as many beautiful and peaceful destinations. It would be difficult to experience a more serene sight than a sunset over the Sea of Japan as seen from the coast of Shimane Prefecture (left). Nor could most people fail to be charmed by the sight of a colorful pagoda against the backdrop of Nachi Waterfall in Wakayama Prefecture.

For more spiritual visitors, Japan's myriad temples and shrines offer havens of rest, relaxation, and renewal. Most visitors to Kyoto's Ryoanji may be perplexed by the famous garden's austere beauty but few will deny its attraction. The same simple beauty is also visible in many of the country's natural-looking though exquisitely manicured gardens, such as Kenrokuen in the city of Kanazawa.

The natural beauty of Japan is also of such exceptional diversity that it is hard to believe that the sun rising over the pine-clad islands of Matsushima in Miyagi Prefecture is the same as that which nurtures exotic flowers on the subtropical island of Okinawa or alpine flora on Hokkaido's lofty peaks.

Every Japanese has his or her own secret spot, and the foreign visitor, whether short-term or long-term, can also experience the calm and serenity of one of the world's most beautiful countries. The crowds and the noise can be avoided and the result will be enough wonderful memories to last a lifetime—or at least until the visitor's next trip to Nippon.

ABOVE
Near the city of Tokushima, the Kirihataji temple is bedecked in cherry blossoms.

BELOW
The monastery complex on Mount Koya, Wakayama Prefecture, is a major center of Japanese Buddhism.

ABOVE
The twenty-five acres of Kenrokuen, in the city of Kanazawa, form one of the most famous gardens in Japan.

RIGHT
The elegant lines of the Kintaikyo bridge in Iwakuni, Yamaguchi Prefecture, draw thousands of sightseers each year.

ABOVE LEFT
The sacred waterfall of the Kumano Nachi shrine is one of more than forty falls in Wakayama Prefecture's Yoshino–Kumano National Park.

LEFT
Mie Prefecture's *meotoiwa*, the "wedded rocks," represent the deities Izanagi and Izanami, the mythical creators of Japan.

ABOVE
Sunrise over Matsushima, a group of over 260 small islands in Matsushima Bay, Miyagi Prefecture, is considered one of Japan's three most beautiful sights.

RIGHT
Okinawa's lush subtropical climate and plant life are unlike anywhere else in the country.

LAND OF FOLK CRAFTS

Dolls in All Shapes and Styles

As indicated in previous chapters, Japan is a land of myriad climates and terrains that demand different lifestyles and methods of adaptation. It is not surprising, therefore, that it is also a land of diverse folk crafts. Different materials and traditions have resulted in different crafts being produced in different regions. Few crafts show this diversity as clearly as doll making does.

Dolls in Japan are not simply playthings for children, as in the West. Some dolls are thought to bring a bountiful harvest, others to ensure longevity, and yet others to guarantee a good test score. At election time, winning candidates throughout the country are televised painting the eyes into giant papier-mâché *daruma* dolls to celebrate ballot-box victories. Smaller versions of the same *daruma*, which originated in eastern Japan and are now chiefly made in the Kanto area, are given to infants as good-luck charms. Kyushu's *Hakata ningyō* (left), probably the Japanese doll most commonly seen outside the country, is definitely not a toy. Instead, these lovely porcelain figures depict the ultimate in classic Japanese beauty and femininity.

The importance of dolls in Japanese tradition is clearly shown each year at the Hina Matsuri, March 3, when girls display tiers of dolls representing a complete Heian-period court, including emperor and empress, attendants, and musicians, all in ancient dress. These displays, customarily given by parents or grandparents to their daughters, can cost literally thousands of dollars.

There are, of course, dolls made simply as toys for little children, but even these, such as the folded paper *chiyogami ningyō*, often seen in Tokyo, are so beautiful that they make excellent low-priced collectibles and souvenirs.

Few countries can claim a heritage so rich in doll making, or pay so much tribute to the makers themselves, as Japan does. Makers of dolls in Japan are certainly not viewed just as toy makers. This is evident when one considers that masters of the craft are designated Intangible Cultural Properties by the government and popularly referred to as Living National Treasures.

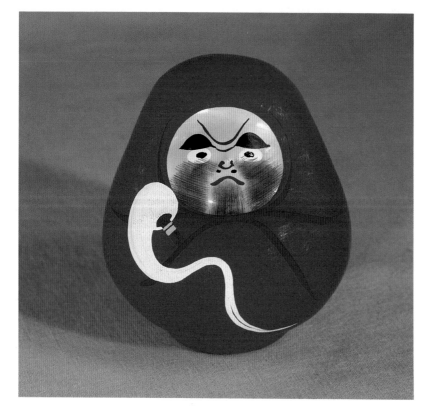

ABOVE
This *daruma* doll from Kanazawa, Ishikawa Prefecture, is thought to bring good luck to the child who receives it.

RIGHT
These *kibigara-zaiku*, straw figures from Tochigi Prefecture, represent the crane and the tortoise, both symbols of longevity.

BELOW RIGHT
This *tenjin-sama* doll from Chiba Prefecture represents the god of education.

BELOW CENTER
Chiyogami paper dolls from Tokyo are still popular toys for children, even in today's electronic world.

BELOW
Kokeshi dolls from Miyagi Prefecture are popular collectibles for tourists and Japanese alike.

ABOVE
This porcelain doll from Nagano Prefecture, holding a bale of rice, is said to assure a good harvest.

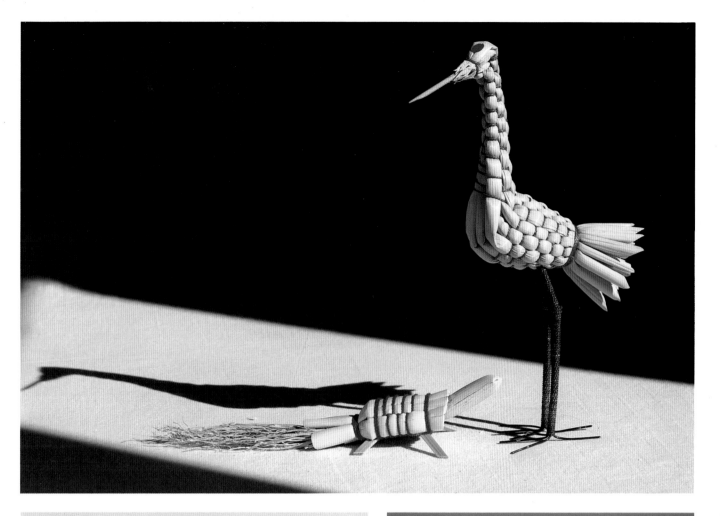